Parenting Survival Guide

The Clever Program for Busy Parents that Want to Raise Happy Children

By

Laura Candice

© **Copyright 2021 by Laura Candice - All rights reserved.**

This document is geared towards providing exact and reliable information in regards to the topic and issue covered. The publication is sold with the idea that the publisher is not required to render accounting, officially permitted, or otherwise, qualified services. If advice is necessary, legal or professional, a practiced individual in the profession should be ordered.

- From a Declaration of Principles, which was accepted and approved equally by a Committee of the American Bar Association and a Committee of Publishers and Associations.

In no way is it legal to reproduce, duplicate, or transmit any part of this document in either electronic means or printed format. Recording of this publication is strictly prohibited, and any storage of this document is not allowed unless with written permission from the publisher. All rights reserved.

The information provided herein is stated to be truthful and consistent. In terms of inattention or otherwise, any liability, by any usage or abuse of any policies, processes, or directions contained within is the solitary and utter responsibility of the recipient reader. Under no

circumstances will take any legal responsibility or blame against the publisher for any reparation, damages, or monetary loss due to the information herein, either directly or indirectly.

Respective authors own all copyrights not held by the publisher.

The information herein is offered for informational purposes solely and is universal as such. The presentation of the information is without a contract or any type of guarantee assurance.

The trademarks used are without any consent, and the publication of the trademark is without permission or backing by the trademark owner. All trademarks and brands within this book are for clarifying purposes only and are owned by the owners themselves, not affiliated with this document.

Author: Laura Candice

Laura Candice is an experience mom of three real kids who live a happy life outside Seattle with her husband. She is also the creator of 7+ incredible works that led her to become a real guru in the field of education between parents and children. Laura has a degree in elementary education, eight years of teaching experience and a pure passion for early childhood learning. Susie's advices have inspired hundreds of thousands of parents through her real, hands-on approach to real parenting.

All her view of life can be summarized in her current motto: "Parents can only give good advice or put it on the right path, but the final formation of a person's character lies in his own hands."

Table of Contents

Introduction 7

CHAPTER 1: Learn to become a Peaceful and Calm Parent .. 13

   1.1 What Happens When You Hit or Scream at Your Child 16

   1.2 Tips for becoming a calmer parent 19

CHAPTER 2: Learn to Raise Confident, Calm, and Happy Children 47

   2.1 Teach your kid constructive psychological habits that create happiness 51

   2.2 Teach your child self-management routines 51

   2.3 Cultivate fun 52

   2.4 Model positive self-talk 53

   2.5 Cultivate optimism 53

   2.6 Have fun as a family, often 61

   2.7 Prioritizing your marriage above your kids 62

   2.8 When your kids speak to you, offer them your full attention 63

   2.9 Have meals together 64

   2.10 Teach your kids to cope with their emotions 64

   2.11 Set boundaries for your kids 66

   2.12 Make sure that your kids get reasonable sleep 67

   2.13 Emphasis on the procedure, not the finished result 69

   2.14 Provide your kids some time to play 69

   2.15 Help solve the issue in your marriage 74

   2.16 Encourage a healthy body 76

2.17 Listen 88

2.18 Make errors when they are looking 89

2.19 Let children make mistakes and messes 90

CHAPTER 3: Discipline your kids 92

CHAPTER 4: Strategies for Building Trust and Attachment 102

4.1 Be Dependable 103

4.2 Be Attentive 104

4.3 Be Predictable 104

4.4 Be Understanding During Separation 105

4.5 Love 106

4.6 Communicate 106

CHAPTER 5: Tips for Inflexible children 110

5.1 Authenticate your child's experience and emotions 111

5.2 Set the boundary peacefully and lovingly 111

5.3 Demonstrate perspective-taking 112

5.4 Model flexibility 113

5.5 Recognize and give positive comments when your kid is flexible 114

Conclusion 116

Introduction

For parents, the well-being of children is more important than almost anything else. More than two-thirds of adults state they are "extremely concerned" about children's well-being, and this concern cuts across ethnicity, education, race, age, and political affiliation. Different people would advise you on raising smart children and successful children, but how do you raise happy children, particularly if you have a very busy lifestyle in which it is incredibly difficult for you to spare your children enough quality time. It's tough sometimes to reconcile what's right for kids and what makes them comfortable, but the two don't have to be mutually exclusive. It is undeniable that happy children are more likely to become successful and accomplished adults. You have to make yourself happy as a first step in the path of raising happier children. You should also encourage your child to respect and develop good relationships. A significant consideration in this regard is that you must not expect phenomenal results from your children, or your children will be overwhelmed and become inactive by ambitious expectations. Consequently, in their lifetime, they would not be able to do something significant and end up in any form of psychiatric illness. Raise a positive child if you just want to give your kids a gift that will accompany them all their lives. This is not always convenient, and it can complicate life. Yet, a positive outlook, no matter what the future holds, will transform life. Positive thoughts contribute to good energy, and the world surrounding you, besides the other people you draw into your life, is heavily affected by your energy. A happy kid looks differently at life and sees the glass half full vs. half empty, which does well for their view on life. Start the day by laughing at your kids and sometimes asking them what made them happy throughout the day. Smiling is infectious and induces a sense of pleasure. Make a deliberate attempt to smile at their response and express approval as your children answer your questions about their day. With optimistic affirmations, greet children. Hello handsome. Sweet girl, good morning. As easy as it sounds, the good feeling that keeps our family united and happy is promoted by special greetings. In bustling family life, it is also a small means of giving approval and affection. Offer sincere praise to them. If your kids do something noteworthy, remember it, no matter how big or small. Do not overdo this. And don't make it up. Look for genuine ways to speak about their success & build up their confidence. Love them as they fail, unconditionally. We want to safeguard our children, as parents, from failing. Yet, failure is part of the learning process and life. Let your children know that you love them, you value them, and that any mistake does not weaken your affection and an optimistic attitude. Encourage your kid to keep a diary. At any age, journaling may begin. Encourage them to write about their experiences in a journal. But let them pick a word of their own. Also, expose the children to the notion of bullet journaling as a way to set their own targets. You can have dinner together. Often this one is difficult. Yet, finding time to spend together every day offers a chance for your children to interact with the family unit. As they grow, the connection will be so vital to them. To talk, be open. That's when your children want to talk. Put the phone down as soon as possible, move away from the dishes, sit down and talk to them. With them, laugh. Tell them all the ways in which they are unique and special. Perhaps the most important thing that you can do to raise a happy and positive kid is to model yourself with a positive attitude. That begins with self-care and respect for oneself. Children will learn from the behavior who see their parents respect themselves. Do you view yourself with respect as a person? When you fail, do you offer yourself grace? Can you find ways for your family to be connected? Are you looking for opportunities to laugh and smile, even on tough days? First, model them in your own life if you want your children to be confident and happy.

CHAPTER 1: Learn to become a Peaceful and Calm Parent

Two of the recognized universal human emotions are rage and frustration, but that doesn't mean that you have to be a victim of bad feelings. We have a responsibility to our families and ourselves as adults to stop allowing our emotions to get the best of us. Let's face it. Parenting is challenging. It can be extremely irritating when you just want to pee alone or take a shower for longer than two minutes without hearing tiny footsteps outside the curtain. Or, if you've told your child to turn off the light as they leave a room for the gazillionth time, it might make you want to pull out your hair. Parents usually manifest their anger and frustration by screaming at their children. It's not that they really want to, but because they get so distracted at times, they lose control. Sometimes, hollering might just be better than learning techniques to become a calmer parent. Studies say that shouting makes kids angrier, emotionally and verbally. Raising your voice to the point of yelling, as an adult, scares kids and makes them feel nervous. Long-term symptoms have been found to be induced as a result of shoutings, such as anxiety, decreased self-esteem, and increased aggression. A calm parent is calming and, in lieu of negative conduct, helps children feel cherished and welcomed. When faced with a circumstance that makes your blood boil, there are many answers that you can choose. Peace-finding is possible. Every parent often gets mad at his or her kids. It doesn't help that life's relentless pressures are still there: meetings we're late for, stuff we've missed at the last minute, financial and health concerns—the list is endless. Our kid, who lost her shoes, randomly recalled that she wanted a new school notebook today, mocked her little brother, or was outright belligerent in the midst of the tension. And we're snapping. In our most relaxed times, if we are honest, we know that, from a state of calm, we can handle any parenting task much better. Yet we remain righteously entitled to our wrath in the storm of our rage. How could this child be so reckless, disregardful, ungrateful, or even mean? Your child can be playing with your shirt buttons, but your reaction is not being triggered by him. Any dilemma which makes you feel like lashing out has its origins in your past. We know this because, in those times, we lose our capacity to think properly, and we start behaving like kids ourselves, showing tantrums. Don't be scared. It's natural, that way. We all reach to the parenting relationship wounded from our babyhoods in every way, and those entire wounds surface with our children. We can expect our children to behave in ways that often drive us off a cliff. As an adult, it is our duty to keep away from the cliff.

1.1 What Happens When You Hit or Scream at Your Child

Imagine your wife or husband losing their patience and shout at you. Now suppose that they are three times the size of you, standing over you. Suppose that for your food, accommodation, safety, security, and you depend on that person entirely. Imagine that they are your only source of affection, self-confidence, and world knowledge, that you have nowhere else to turn. Take whatever passions you have summoned and multiply them by a factor of 1000 now. That's almost like what happens to your kid inside when you get mad at him. All of us, of course, get mad at our kids and, sometimes, furious. The objective is to depend on our adulthood so that we manage and thus mitigate the negative effects of the expression of anger. Rage is terrifying enough. Calling a name or other vocal abuse, in which the adult talks rudely to the kid, takes an advanced personal toll, as the child depends on the parent for his or her own sense of self. And it has been shown that children who experience physical violence, like spanking, have lifelong adverse consequences that stretch to every corner of their adult lives, from decreased IQ to stormy marriages to a greater risk of drug misuse. It's an indicator that he/she has seen so much of it and has built barriers against it and against you that your young child now does not seem afraid of your wrath. The tragic consequence is a kid who is less likely to try to act to impress you and who is more open to the peer group's pressures, meaning you have to do some restoration work. Our rage is nothing short of alarming to our children, whether or not they show it, and the more often we get upset, the more they will be defended and perhaps less likely to show it.

1.2 Tips for becoming a calmer parent

Since you are human, often you will find yourself in the mode of "fight or flight," and your child will begin to look like an enemy. We are actually ready to fight when we're swept away by indignation. Our bodies are flooded with neurotransmitters and hormones. They trigger stress in your muscles, your pulse to fight, and your breath to get faster. At those moments, it's hard to keep cool, but we all know that smacking our children—while it can offer immediate relief—is not exactly what we need to do. The most critical thing about rage to remember is NOT to act when you're angry. You will feel an intense need to act, to give a lesson to your child. But that is your rage that is doing the talking. It thinks it's an emergency. Though, it nearly never is. Later, you will teach your boy, and it will be moral that you really want to teach. It's not your child going somewhere. You know where she's living.

So pledge now to NO beating, no cursing, and no naming your child's names while upset. What about cursing? That's a tantrum, never at your kids. If you just need to yell, get the windows turned up in your car and shout so no one can listen, and do not use words because they make you madder. Just shout. Your kids get upset, too, but seeking positive means to deal with your frustration is a double gift to them: not only do you not harm them, but you also offer them a role model. From time to time, your child can probably see you upset and how you treat them, such circumstances tell kids a lot. Can you show your kid the right thing to do? Will parents still have tantrums? Is this yelling the way adults cope with conflict? If so, as a measure of how sensible they are, they'll adopt these traits. Or would you model for your kid that rage is part of being human and that it is part of being an adult to learn to handle anger responsibly? Using the following techniques, learn to control your anger & arrive at a peaceful solution:

Study the negative effects of showing anger

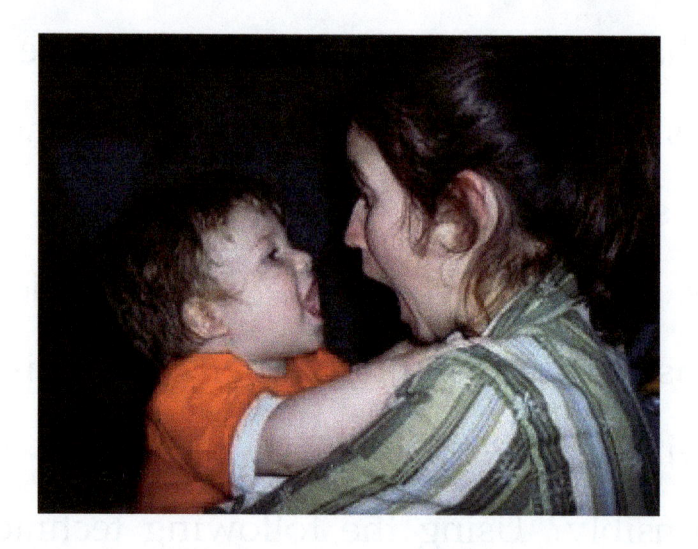

In the short-term, it is tempting to go with your frustration, but giving in to frustration will cause far more problems. Consider how it will be after the smoke clears before lashing out at your kids or doing what you considered to be acceptable actions.

Cool yourself down before you take any step

You need a way to cool down when you get this mad. Awareness is only going to help you tackle your self-control and adjust your physiology: pause, drop and inhale. That deep breath provides you with a decision. Would you really want the feelings to be hijacked? Remind yourself now that there is no emergency. Shake out the tension of your hands. Take 10 more breaths. You should try to find a way to be happy, which will relieve the anxiety and change the mood. Even pushing yourself to grin gives your nervous system a reminder that there is no emergency, and it begins to calm you down. Suppose a noise has to be made, hum. It will help discharge your anger emotionally, so you should try to put on some song and dance. If you can get 20 minutes in a day for practice of mindfulness, you can potentially build the neural ability so that in these times of frustration, it is easier to calm down. But even everyday life with kids can give you lots of chances to learn, and you renew your mind so that you have extra self-control whenever you resist behaving when you're irritated. Some people do take the timeworn recommendation to clobber a pillow, so it's better that you can do that sort of discharge in private because it can be frightening for your kid to watch you stuff the pillow. This is a controversial technique because evidence shows that striking something settles to your body that this is really an emergency, and you can remain in "fight or flight." So it can dress you out, but it does not get to the emotions that fuel the agitation and can only make you madder. Instead, if you can breathe slowly and accept angry emotions, you would probably find that there is anxiety, depression, disappointment right under the frustration. Let yourself feel those emotions, and the anger will melt away. Timeouts aren't for small children either. To cool down, adults also need timeouts or brief breaks. Give yourself a few minutes by taking deep breaths to allow a level of rationality to return to your mind. In order to make appropriate parental decisions, you'll be in a better place.

When appropriate, let your family members be wrong

It's not your job to prove anyone is wrong; just let them be wrong. This is the ego barking when you have a deep need to convince them that they're mistaken. Of course, as a mom, it is your duty to teach your kids about right and wrong. However, at the end of the day, you cannot control the decisions they make, and inevitably, they will have to learn from the repercussions when they suffer judgment errors.

Decide which is more important: being happy or being right

Most arguments are the product of the desire to be correct. Your life will be more fun, and you will become a more comfortable parent overall if you choose to be happy about winning any heated debate with your children. What is more important to you?

Take a minute to notice your anger

Instead of listening to your anger mindlessly, take a minute to analyze it. Pretend that you're a third party experiencing your frustration and discomfort. How does it feel to you like? Where in your body is the feeling coming from? Does your head, chest, or stomach have the feeling? Has it affected your breathing? Are your hands clenching or shaking? You will achieve a new outlook and weaken your negative feelings by disengaging from your anger.

Ask yourself why you're upset

Has anyone hurt you physically? Were you let down by them? Breach one of your values? Figure out that you are upset because, in order to find a solution, you will be able to take the appropriate steps.

Focus on the big picture

Just imagine that you learned the next Friday, the world would come to an end. If your kid did not hang his knapsack, would you be upset? Not of course.

Search for answers instead of trying to make you feel better

Acting in a rage is about making you feel better. For example, rather than shouting at your kids, focus on finding a peaceful solution. The effect is going to be a lot smoother and well worth the time.

Be sure you understand the situation

Why get furious at your children before you know the facts? Be sure the problem isn't a potential miscommunication.

Learn and practice relaxation techniques

As an adult, the happier you are on a daily basis, the less likely you will get upset. Techniques of calming can also be useful after the fact. Learn to self-calm yourself. It is an ability that can be learned.

See your annoyance as a practice opportunity to find peace

See the scenario as an opportunity to exercise your anger-management skills each time you feel frustrated. In disguise, it's a blessing. Commit yourself to treat this bit of anger better than the last time you did it. Stop letting the best of you overcome by your anger, annoyance, and frustrations. You have choices open to you as a thoughtful, caring human being and father. Rather than give in to the immediate desires, strive to find answers and peace.

Set limits before you get angry

Sometimes, when we get irritated about our kids, it's because we haven't set a limit, and there's something grating on us. It's a warning to do something the minute you start feeling mad, no, not yelling. To stop more of whatever conduct is irritating you, engage in a constructive way. If your frustration stems from you, let's presume you have had a hard day, and you are totally worn out because of your hectic schedule. It might help illustrate this to your kids and remind them to be considerate and keep in control of, at least for now, the behavior that irritates them. If the kids are doing anything that is extremely annoying—playing a game in which somebody is likely to get injured, stalling after you've asked them to do anything, squabbling when you're on the phone—you might need to interfere with what you are doing, repeat your demands, and readdress them, to prevent the problem from worsening, and your rage.

Take Five

Identify that in any case, an upset state is a horrible starting point to interfere. Give yourself a break instead and return back when you feel relaxed. Physically, step away from your kid so that you will not be desirous of reaching out to touch him violently. Only say, as politely as you can, 'Right now, I'm too mad to talk about this. I'm going to take a break to calm myself down.

Exiting doesn't cause the child to win. It makes them impressed with how serious the offense is, and it models self-control. Utilize this time not to work yourself into yet another rage over how correct you are but to relax. You should go into the shower, put some water on your face, and breathe. You should do this only if your kid is old enough to be left behind for a moment. But if your child is young to feel lost, they'll pursue you crying as you leave. (This can be accomplished even by certain adult couples. If you cannot leave your kid without increasing their rage, go to the sink and wash your hands. Then relax for a few minutes on the sofa with your child, breathe deeply and say a little hymn that repairs your calm, including one of these:

"This is not a disaster."

"Children want to love most when they need it least."

"He's behaving in this particular manner only because he wants my help with his feelings."

It's all right to say your mantra loudly. With your children, it's nice role modeling to see you cope responsibly with the big attitudes. Don't be shocked if your kid picks up your word and begins doing it while he's upset.

Instead of acting on it, listen to your rage

Rage is as much a given as our legs and arms, like most emotions. What we are in possession of is what we want to do with it. For us, anger also provides a powerful lesson, but behaving when we're angry is rarely constructive, even in extreme circumstances involving self-defense, so we make decisions from a reasonable state that we might never make. The productive way to deal with frustration is to restrict our expression of it and to utilize it diagnostically while we cool down: whatever is wrong with our lives that we feel upset, and what do we have to do to change the condition? Often the solution is directly linked to our parenting: before everything gets out of control, we need to enforce rules or begin getting the kids to bed thirty minutes earlier and/or do some sorts of mending work on our relationship with our kid so that she stops her rude behavior with us. Often we're shocked to discover that our dissatisfaction is really with our partner who doesn't behave like a complete parenting partner or even our employer. And maybe the reason is that we're holding out the frustration that we don't know spills out on our children, and we need to get assistance by counseling or the support group of the parents.

Remember that "showing" your anger to other people can reinforce and intensify it

There is nothing positive about showing anger "at" another person, despite the common belief that we need to "show" our anger, so it doesn't eat away at us. Research reveals that it simply makes us more annoyed to show rage when we are angry. In fact, this leaves the other one hurt and frightened, so they get more agitated. Not unexpectedly, this develops the gap in the relationship instead of fixing anything. What's more, voicing rage is not always authentic. Rage is an assault on the other guy because inside, you feel so distressed. True authenticity will communicate the hurt or insecurity that gives rise to the annoyance that you may have with a partner. But for your child, managing your own feelings is your responsibility, not imposing them on your kid, so you must be more cautious. The solution is always to first settle down. Then, before you make choices about what to say and do, consider what the deeper "message" of anger is.

Wait before disciplining

Make it a point to never, though upset, take any action. You have to simply say such things as:

"I can't believe that after we've spoken about how beating hurts, you still cannot stop hitting your brother. I must think about this, and this afternoon, we'll talk about it. I want you to be on your good behavior then. In order to relax down, take a 10-minute break. Don't revise the situation in your mind — it will only make you angrier. Use the following methods, instead, to relax down. But if you've taken a 10-minute break to relate constructively and still don't feel relaxed enough, do not hesitate to put the conversation off:

I would like to think about what happened, and we're going to talk more about it. I need to prepare dinner in the meantime, and you must complete your homework, please.'

Sit with your kid after dinner and, if possible, define firm boundaries. But you would be more capable of listening to his side of things and reacting to his behavior with fair, respectful, enforceable limits.

Avoid physical power

Nearly 85 percent of teenagers claim that their parents have hit or spanked them. And still, study after study has found that hitting and other physical measures have a life-long detrimental effect on the well-being of children. The American Academy of Pediatrics explicitly warns against it. What we need to think about is that if the adult depression and anxiety crisis of our society are in part triggered by the aftermath of too many of us growing up with adults who abused us. The physical violence is minimized by many parents they have suffered due to the emotional hurt is too severe to acknowledge. Yet, repressing childhood trauma just makes us more likely to smash our own kids. Spanking can momentarily make you feel better because it releases your anger, but it's horrible for your kids and actually sabotages all the good things you do as a parent. Hitting has a way of increasing along with even slapping. There's also some proof that the parent is addicted to spanking, and it gives you a chance to release that rage and feel better. However, there are safer options for you to feel good, so your child won't get upset. To control yourself, do whatever you must do, including leaving the room. If you can't manage yourself and end up succumbing to the use of physical strength, apologize and reassure your kid that it's never okay to strike and get some help for yourself.

Avoid threats

Threats made while you're mad are always going to be unreasonable. As threats are effective only if you are ready to follow them through, they diminish your right and make it less likely that next time your children will follow the directions. Alternatively, tell your kid that you have to think about a suitable response to this breach of the directions. The suspense is going to be severe than listening to a chain of threats that they know you are not going to enforce.

Check your word choice and tone

Research indicates that the more we speak calmly, the more we feel relaxed, and the more calmly we react to others. Similarly, the use of harsh words or other emotional words makes us more irritated with our listeners, and the situation gets out of control. In our own tone of voice and use of words, we have the ability to relax or annoy ourselves and the one with whom we are communicating. You have to keep in mind one thing, and that is "You are the real Role Model."

Still angry

Don't get close to the anger. Let go of it once you've heard it and did adequate adjustments. If this doesn't work, bear in mind that rage is always protection. It defends us from becoming vulnerable. Look at the pain or insecurity underneath the rage to get rid of the anger. Perhaps you're scared of your son's tantrums, or your daughter's so obsessed with her mates that she's unconcerned about the family, and that's hurting you. Your rage will dissipate once you recognize the underlying feelings and let yourself sense them. And you're going to be more likely to intervene with your kid constructively to resolve what felt like an impossible task.

Create and share a list of healthy ways to cope with anger

You should speak to your children about healthy ways to cope with rage when things in your house are normal. Is it ever all right to hit somebody? Is throwing things all right? Is it alright to shout? Remember that because you are ideal, you are still subject to the laws that implement on your child. Next, list together appropriate ways of coping with rage and post it on your fridge so it can be read daily by all in the house. When you start to get crazy, let your children see you check it.

"Express the other person whatever you need without being offensive."

"Turn on songs and dance out your anger."

"Whenever you want to smack, pat your hands around your body and grip yourself."

Pick your battles

Your precious relationship capital is drained with any unpleasant encounter with your kids. Focus on how other people are treated by your child. His coat on the floor might make you mad in the broader scheme of things, but it's not worth getting your relationship account in the red over. Know that the more your connection with your kid is optimistic and interactive, the more he is going to follow your way.

Think you are part of the issue

Your kid will always teach you where you must focus on yourself if you are open to emotional development. It's difficult to be a nonviolent parent if you are not, and something will prompt you to act your nastiest. We have the ability to relax or intensify the situation in any encounter with our child. It may be that your child behaves in ways that make you worse, but you are not a powerless victim. Next, take responsibility for managing your own feelings. Your child does not become a small angel immediately, but if you learn to keep calm in the face of her rage, you'll be shocked to see how much less angry your child responds.

Keep searching for appropriate ways to discipline which facilitate better conduct

There are much more efficient forms of disciplining than violence, and, in fact, evidence indicates that disciplining with rage creates a loop that facilitates wrongdoing. Some parents are shocked to learn that, even with punishments or timeouts, there are homes where kids are not disciplined, and parental shouting is rare. Of course, boundaries are set, and there are behavioral guidelines, but they are enforced by the relationship between parent and child and through supporting kids with the desires and distresses that motivate their' bad' behavior. The study is obvious that these families make a child who, at a younger age, take greater responsibility for his actions and are the emotionally best-adjusted.

If you deal with your frustration sometimes, pursue therapy

There is no embarrassment in calling for assistance. The shame lies in defaulting on your duty as a parent by physically or mentally harming your child.

CHAPTER 2: Learn to Raise Confident, Calm, and Happy Children

Raising happier kids is the holy grail of parental success for many parents. But we believe satisfaction is all too much in those brief seconds of having what you want, too. Actually, enduring happiness is much more challenging and a lot more satisfying. And yes, you will boost the odds of your child being happy significantly, simply from the way you parent him or her. What helps a happier kid mature into a happy grown-up? As happiness is a by-product of mental well-being. You will learn in this chapter is about helping you raise a happier child, from meeting your child's need to be soothed to helping your child grow in confidence. So let's talk about what makes humans happy, specifically. The new happiness study offers us fascinating responses. Once survival, stability, and essential comforts are guaranteed, our level of enjoyment is not disturbed much by external circumstances. Our genes undoubtedly help in raising our satisfaction set points to a higher degree. Our own behavioral, emotional, and physical patterns, which establish the body chemistry that defines our level of happiness, turn out to be the largest determinant of our happiness. We both know that some of us have a more cheerful disposition than others. Some of this is innate, only the destiny of the genes that give us a happy environment. Most of our mood, though, is a behavior. Seeing pleasure as a habit can sound strange. Yet it is possible that we have fallen into the habit of always being happy, or the habit of being mostly sad, by the time we're adults. Three kinds of habits are closely correlated with happiness:

How we learn of the world and feel, and thus interpret our perceptions.

Certain activities or routines, such as daily exercise, balanced food, reflection, communicating with other people, and smiling and laughing regularly.

Character qualities such as self-control, fairness, caring for others, citizenship, intelligence, bravery, management, and loyalty.

In practice, certain character traits are simply habits; when faced with certain kinds of circumstances, tendencies to behave in certain ways. And it definitely makes sense that the more these qualities we display, the more our lives function, the better we feel about ourselves, and the more value we find in life. The ways Grandma taught us we should live are some of the behaviors that build happiness: work hard, respect relationships with other people, keep our bodies safe, treat our money responsibly and contribute to our society. Others are more personal self-management habits, such as controlling our moods and cultivating optimism, that insulate us from unhappiness and generate joy in our lives. But they become ingrained and serve a defensive role once we make those behaviors part of our lives. The tips and tactics for raising happier kids are listed below:

2.1 Teach your kid constructive psychological habits that create happiness

You have to teach constructive behaviors to your children, such as mood management, positive self-talk, being hopeful, enjoying life, practicing gratitude, and cherishing our connectedness with each other and the world as a whole. Build these together in your life so that you constantly model them, learn about using them, and you will be copied by your kids.

2.2 Teach your child self-management routines

Daily exercises, balanced eating, and meditation are all closely associated with levels of satisfaction. But you and your child will have more personal techniques of their own; music is an instant mood lifter for certain individuals, and a walk-in nature still works for some.

2.3 Cultivate fun

The old saying that the greatest cure is humor turns out to be true. The more we smile, the happier we become. Literally, it affects our chemistry in the body. So the next time you and your kid try to shake the doldrums off, how about a movie about the Marx brothers? And here's a great tool: smiling makes us happy, even though we force it at first. The input from our facial muscles reminds us that we are pleased, and our mood increases automatically. Not to mention the moods of everyone around us—so that everybody is uplifted by the feedback loop.

2.4 Model positive self-talk

We just need a cheerleader to get us through the various challenges in life. Who's saying that we can't be our own? Really, who's better? Research shows that happier people offer continuing reassurance, appreciation, praise, and pep talks to themselves. Speak to yourself aloud, like someone you love, so that your children can hear you.

2.5 Cultivate optimism

Optimism defends against disappointment. Some of us, it's true, are born more positive than others, but we can all nurture this.

Help your child find joy in everyday things

Studies suggest that people who appreciate, and encourage themselves to be touched by the little miracles of everyday life, are happier.

In our example, children understand what's important in life.

Support your child to prioritize relationships

Studies reveal that throughout their lives, people who are comfortable have more people and closer connections with such persons. Teach your child that they're worth it when relationships take up work.

Help your child develop gratitude

We seem to forget that happiness doesn't come in when we get what we don't have, but rather because we understand and enjoy what we have. Many people feel that until they are satisfied, they can't be thankful, implying until they have anything to be grateful for. But look closely, and you'll find that it's the opposite: when they are grateful, people are happy.

People who identify themselves as deliberately fostering gratitude are rated both by those who know them and by themselves as happier. Children don't have a life context because they don't know whether they're lucky or unlucky, only that their friend has more expensive shoes. Yet, there are also ways to make kids learn to develop gratitude, which is the reverse of taking all for granted.

Accept all emotions

Life is full of love, but life is also full of suffering and sadness for even the happiest human, and we have everyday causes to grieve, great and small. It's not focusing on the negative to understand our sad emotions, and it's exposing up to the full range of being human. In reality, acknowledging those awkward, sad feelings deepen our capacity to take pleasure in our lives. So deciding to be happy doesn't mean that our emotions are being repressed. It means remembering all our emotions and respecting them, and making ourselves believe them. That encourages us to move through the emotions, so they begin to dissolve. Simply empathizing with your child with her distressed feelings will allow her to feel them, which will enable the feelings to start to evaporate so that she can move on. This is not a phase that can be rushed, so you should be quite magnanimous in giving your child the desired time that he needs.

Help him learn how to manage his moods

Most people don't know that they can choose to let go of bad moods and alter their moods consciously. But practice can really make us happier by doing this. This can be practiced through:

Monitoring moods

Allowing oneself to express the desires while holding oneself in love

Notice any negative thoughts which give rise to feelings. ("My child shouldn't be acting this way. He'll grow up to be a terrible person if he does this!")

By choosing a thought that makes you feel a bit better. (For example, "My child is acting like a child as he is a child. My child won't always be like this.")

Of course, the hard part is choosing a bad mood to change. It's hard to take constructive action to change things while you're at it. There's no reason for you to go from desolate to cheerful. Only find a way to make you feel a bit happier for yourself. That empowers you to actually face, and try to solve, what's upsetting you. Occasionally, simply changing our way of thinking about a problem changes things. So instead of "How can my child be nasty to me like that, with all I do for him?!" you might want to do that for him. "It's common for kids to get angry at their parents. This is because my child is struggling right now, and he wants me to try to understand him." How can your child help with her moods? Talk to her about strategies for getting into a better mood sometimes when she's in a good mood: what works for her? Share with your child whatever works for you. Then, if she's in a bad mood, start with empathy. Ask her whether she needs help to change her attitude after she has had some time to feel her anger. Even if, initially, she can only choose a better mood one out of ten times, she will soon begin to notice how much better her life works when she does it.

Counteract the message that happiness can be bought

We need to realize, as adults, that we are not the only ones who educate our children about life. They get the relentless advertising message that more money and more stuff are the goals of life. Ultimately, it's going to matter what we teach them, but we need to specifically confront those destructive signals.

Help your child learn the joy of contribution

Evidence demonstrates that the pride in contributing to society's progress makes us happy, and it will also make our kids happier. Our task as parents is to find opportunities for them to make a meaningful difference in the world so that they can appreciate this opportunity and benefit from it.

Be a happier person

Parents' emotional issues are related to their children's emotional problems. Not just that, depressed persons are less successful parents as well. Philip Cowan and Carolyn, psychologists, have both observed that happier parents are more likely to have glad kids. Children were asked in a study in The Secrets of Happy Families: "If you had one wish for your parents, what would it be?" No, it was not that they would pass more time with their parents. Nor was it that their parents were less likely to nag at them or allow them more liberty. The wish for the children for their parents was that they wanted their parents to be less depressed and stressed. So what would you do to make yourself a happy individual? Please continue the reading to find the answer to this mind-boggling question.

2.6 Have fun as a family, often

Both little and big things are celebrated by happy families: the end of a hectic week, a good score, the first day at school, a job promotion, vacations, and eves. The festivities can be as easy as going together to the park or as descriptive as arranging a surprise get-together. Happy families produce happy kids, so make it a habit to often party as a family.

2.7 Prioritizing your marriage above your kids

Exhausted, Anxious, and demanding parents, entitled children are created by families focused on children. Today, parents are so fast to risk our lives and our marriages for our kids." Having a fulfilling marriage is the utmost gift you can give your kids. Given below are some easy tips to support your marriage:

Embrace twice a day

Welcome each other happily

Congratulate one another

Hold hands frequently

Have regular night outs

Spend 20 minutes each day in conversation

Say every day, "I love you."

2.8 When your kids speak to you, offer them your full attention

If you want them to be successful and happy, communicating well with your kids is vital. Whenever they speak to you, one successful way of doing this is to provide your full attention to them. It means putting your journals and electrical devices aside and hearing what they want to say. You are going to respond more carefully; that will encourage your kids to be more communicative.

2.9 Have meals together

In school and in almost every area, kids who have meals with their relatives become more successful. These kids have greater language skills, greater confidence in themselves, and better marks. They are less likely to smoke, drink, do drugs, or developmental problems as well. And this all is because these families have lunchtimes together frequently.

2.10 Teach your kids to cope with their emotions

The study indicates that kids who can control their emotions concentrate better, which is essential for enduring success. Even these kids enjoy healthier physical health. In order to support your kids manage their feelings, you should:

- Exhibit yourself emotional self-management
- Understand your kids
- Teach your kids that all emotions are okay, but not all habits are acceptable.
- Acknowledge the progress of your kids
- Teach your kids to form significant relationships

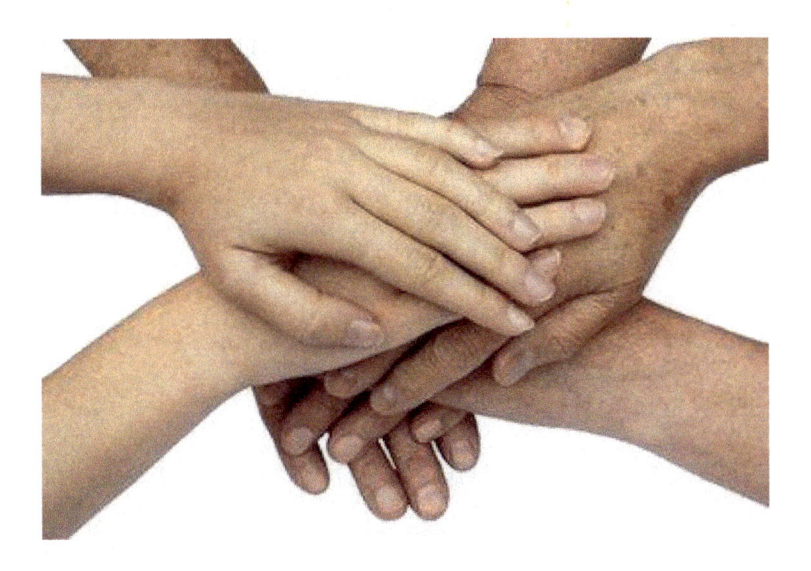

Studies have found that for the development and mental well-being of children, having strong relationships is vital. Kids who lack these connections do much worse school, have difficulties with the law, and have psychological issues. What can parents do to support their children in forming significant relationships? Parents should respond to the emotional signs of their children appropriately. Their kids will feel safer by doing so. The basis of self-esteem is established by this. Parents must build an environment to make friendships with their children while teaching them to fix disputes as well.

2.11 Set boundaries for your kids

Parents who set and implement clear limits raise children who are positive and effective. Dr. Linda Caldwell and Dr. Nancy Darling also discovered that productive parents demonstrate to their children the logic of the laws. They teach the children the values behind the directions. In doing so, they develop a closer bond with their kids that is more compassionate. About parents that do not set limits, Darling says: "... children take the absence of directions as a symbol that their parents don't really care that their parents don't really want this job of being a parent." It's dangerous to feel too regulated as a parent. But to make the best of their potential, kids need limits.

2.12 Make sure that your kids get reasonable sleep

Research reveals that kids who do not get enough sleep:

Have lower brain output

Can't concentrate well

They are more likely to be overweight

Less innovative

They are less likely to control their thoughts

This is quite a scary list. Establish a regular bedtime schedule and restrict distracting activity after dinner in order to help your kids get enough sleep. In addition, within 1 - 2 hours of bedtime, don't permit screen time. This is due to disturbed sleep cycles by the blue light emitting from electronic devices, and melatonin development is impaired. To improve their sleep efficiency, you should even keep your children's bedroom as comfortable and dim as possible.

2.13 Emphasis on the procedure, not the finished result

Parents who exaggerate success are more likely to bring up kids who have mental issues and involve in dangerous behavior. What is the alternative to insisting on accomplishment, then? Concentrate on the system. A study by Dr. Carol Dweck indicates that kids who focus on commitment and mindset, not on the intended goal, end up having more achievement in the long run. So watch out for ways to appreciate the positive conduct, mood, and effort of your kids. With the passage of time, they can produce improved results eventually.

2.14 Provide your kids some time to play

You don't refer to arcade games or iPads when you say "play." You are pointing to unstructured playtime, ideally outdoors. Playtime is crucial for the learning and development of children. The study also reveals that the less unstructured playtime kids get, the more likely they are to have physical, cognitive, social, and behavioral well-being developmental problems. Having a playful attitude is also connected to superior academic achievement. So offer more unstructured playtime to your kids, and they'll become healthier students. This will not, of course, make them into straight-A students on their own, but playing is necessary for their progress.

Reduce your children's TV time

There is a strong correlation between improved satisfaction and less Television time. In other words, happy individuals watch less Television than sad individuals. A survey of over 4,000 teens showed that it was more likely that someone who watched more Television would become depressed. With more Television time, this chance has arisen. By restricting your own TV time, set a precedent for your kids. To decide on your family's TV-watching rules, you should even have a family conversation.

Encourage the children to maintain a diary of appreciation

Maintaining a gratitude journal will raise your satisfaction rate by 25 percent within just ten weeks. The people who maintain a gratitude diary are not only happier, they often have more optimism for the future and less frequently feel ill. How would you start keeping a record of gratitude? Phase 1: Grab a notepad and pen, then put them on the table at your bedside. Step 2: Write down two or three items every night before you go to sleep that what you're grateful for. "Here are some samples of what you might write: (Don't think about how "large" or "little" these things are.)

Good health

Loving friends and relatives

Awesome sunset

Delightful chicken stew for dinner

Smooth traffic

Enable your kids to make their own decisions

There are many advantages of letting kids schedule their own timelines and set their own targets. Such children are more likely to be organized and concentrated, and in the future, to make wiser choices. Moreover, letting their children pick their own penalties is helpful for parents. Kids who do so less often violate the rules. Allow your children, wherever possible, to choose their own deeds too. Dr. Rich Gilman found that children who partake in organized school events selected by them are 24% more likely to love going to school. So, when your kids grow older, allow them the opportunity to make more decisions on their own. As a result, they'll become successful and happier.

2.15 Help solve the issue in your marriage

Kids whose parents have significant marriage issues do poorer academically and are more expected to use drugs and/or alcohol. Furthermore, these children are more expected to have emotional difficulties. It must not surprise anyone. There are a large number of families in which parents have big marriage difficulties that are continuing. This undoubtedly affects children, who are less inspired, accountable, and involved. Please seek support from a doctor or psychologist if you have difficulties with your marriage that have not been resolved for years or months. Your kids and your marriage rely on you.

Motivate your kids to help others and to be kind

The study of children of age 8 - 12 by Dr. Mark Holder shows that kids who feel like their lives are expressive are often happier. What makes them see their lives as something more meaningful? For example, as they support other persons, they make a difference in the world, volunteering, help their friends and families. As discovered by Dr. L. B. Aknin, being generous often makes children happy. She observed that when they give away small gifts to others, children are happier than when they accept treats. Interestingly, as they give away sweets that belong to them, instead of the same treats that do not belong to them, children get much happier. To inspire your kids to serve and be charitable to others, and also find opportunities to do this as a family.

2.16 Encourage a healthy body

For girls, having a strong body image is particularly important, although it may also affect boys. 1/3rd of 13-year-old girls are unhappy about their weight, according to a survey undertaken by the Institute of Child Welfare. Furthermore, another study showed that 69 percent of mothers made derogatory remarks in front of their kids about their bodies. This influences the self-image of their children themselves. Here are several ways in which you can help your children foster a healthy body image:

Emphasis on exercise's health benefits rather than how it influences your body.

Pay attention more to improving the character and abilities of your children and less on their physical appearance.

Workout as a family together

Speak to your kids about how the media impacts how we perceive our bodies.

Do not talk about how much you felt guilty after eating specific foods.

Do not make a judgment on the appearance of others.

Don't yell at your kids

Dr. Laura Markham explains how you can easily turn your house into a constant battlefield by shouting at your children. It is more likely that kids who live in such a threatening atmosphere would feel worried and scared. Remove yourself from the situation while you are on the brink of losing your temperament.

Before speaking to your child again, take ten minutes to compose your thoughts. Practice understanding the emotions of your children in a method called "emotion coaching." Suppose that your colleague or manager is there in the room with you if it helps. You will speak more kindly to your kids in this manner.

Teach to forgive

Forgiveness has been described as a central factor that contributes to happiness in children by Dr. Martin Seligman, generally regarded as the founder of positive psychology. Inability to forgive has also been related to anxiety and depression. Kids who learn to forgive are able to turn bad emotions into constructive ones about the past. This raises their pleasure levels and satisfaction with life. For your children, be a role model. Don't keep grudges and take the opportunity to settle personal disputes against persons who have wronged you. Discuss with your children the value of forgiving so that they can transform forgiveness into a lifestyle.

Teach your kids to think confidently

Dr. Seligman also observed, not surprisingly, that kids who are more confident appear to be happier. How do you teach your kids to think positively? One approach is to motivate them to maintain a log of thanks. Below are few more methods:

Create your own optimistic outlook.

Complaining should be avoided

Do not gossip

Don't make a big deal of spilled alcohol, broken dishes, etc.

See and acknowledge the best in others

Tell the children to say something favorably, such as "I like to play with David and Sarah" instead of "I hate to play with Tom."

Tell your kids about the obstacles you face and how those challenges help you grow.

Create a family task statement

Parents are encouraged to create a family mission statement. This statement defines the ideals and mutual vision of your family. Just about any corporation has a mission declaration, and so should your family.

Have family meetings

You should have a twenty-minute family meet-up once a week as a family. During the meeting, you may ask all the family members the 3 questions:

What have you done well in the last week?

What have you struggled to do so well in the last week?

What are you going to focus on next week?

These gatherings can bring the family close together and increase the significance of relationships between families. You will really be excited by attending these sessions. So it is strongly recommended, if you have not already done so, to initiate this practice.

Share your family antiquity with your kids

The study indicates that there are greater levels of self-esteem in kids who know more about their family background. This later in life adds to their prosperity and happiness. Dr. Robyn Fivush and Dr. Marshall Duke have created a "Do You Know" scale, which contains 20 questions about their family background that kids may be able to answer. Will you remember any of the illnesses and accidents your parents encountered when they were younger?" These questions contain "Do you remember any incidents that occurred with your mother or father when they were in college? Sharing the past of your family strengthens family relations and makes your children grow more resilient.

Make family rituals

Family practices, as observed by Dr. Lynda Walters and Dr. Dawn Eaker in their study, improve family cohesiveness and enable children to learn socially. To make these traditions in your home, make a deliberate effort. Some examples are given below:

Having breakfast every Saturday as a family

Play a board game every evening

Cook lunch as a family

Enjoy the joint evening walks

Keep a family meeting every week

Go camping once a year as a family

Spend good time once a month with your children

Support your kids to find a counselor

Dr. Lisa Colarossi also found that kids who have a trustworthy adult in their life (other than their parents) have 30 percent high levels of satisfaction than children who don't. By urging your child to join an association or by login for a mentoring plan, you can find a mentor for your child.

Form Happiness Habits

You may help children build lasting happiness habits. This can be achieved with the help of the following powerful methods, which are backed by research:

Stimulus removal: Remove temptations and distractions out of the way.

Make It Public: State objectives to increase social support — and social pressure.

One Goal at a Time: Numerous goals overwhelm willpower, especially for children. Establish one habit before pursuing another.

Keep at it: You must not expect excellence immediately. It may take time. There will be declines. This is normal. Keep reinforcing.

More Playtime

Most children already practice mindfulness when they play, fully enjoying the present moment. But today's kids spend less time playing both indoors and outdoors... All told, kids have lost eight hours a week of free, unstructured, and spontaneous play over the last two decades. Playtime is important for helping children to grow and learn. Researchers conclude that this drastic decline in unstructured playtime is partially responsible for slowing cognitive and emotional growth for children... In addition to helping children learn to self-regulate, academic, physical, social, and emotional well-being is facilitated by child-led, unstructured play (with or without adults). Unstructured play lets kids learn how to work, share, compromise, settle disputes, manage their thoughts and actions, and stand up for themselves in groups. There are no strict instructions needed here: budget more time for your children to just get out and simply play.

2.17 Listen

Listening to your kid actively involves not interrupting, eye contact, and not waiting for your chance to talk. Don't give it if they aren't querying for advice. Ask them questions Instead, such as, "What do you think you can do with this?" or "How did you feel about it?" It would encourage them to continue engaging by genuinely listening to what your kid needs to tell you. Making each conversation a lesson leaves them feeling disempowered and inferior (especially if the lesson is purposely given by you). Take the benefit of time in the car or at lunch together to practice only listening with a broad mind to their thoughts.

2.18 Make errors when they are looking

Kids learn from your pattern more than they follow your words. They need to see you burn dinner or occasionally fall on the ski slopes if you want them to trust that part of development is doing mistakes. When you make a parenting error, it is one of your most effective chances to show this to your kid. Let's say you're losing your cool and screaming. You can say, "I don't want to shout at you when I'm frustrated," instead of hoping they'll forget your outburst. I apologize. Mommies can also make mistakes.

2.19 Let children make mistakes and messes

Happy kids know they're able to cope. By getting off at the incorrect bus stand or pouring the water too fast and letting it spill, they have learned. Children feel supported when they do not do something correct the first time, and they keep trying, according to child psychologist JoAnn Deak. This contributes to kids as adults with bigger problem-solving abilities. Outside the box, the capacity to think is more about nurture than nature. It translates into success in adulthood when they acquire this style of thinking in infancy.

Offer them wings and watch them flying

Ultimately, our responsibility as parents is to show our kids how to care about their own desires. We think so hard about all the stuff that could go wrong that we strip our children of the chance to try. Start off with easy material. How many times have you turned your child's shower until they are completely able to turn the water on and control the temperature on their own? These are all the beginner's steps for people who are self-supporting and happy. But all starts with a pleased child.

CHAPTER 3: Discipline your kids

The parent must regularly discipline the child. Parents who hold back from providing limits to children or punishing bad behavior firmly (but lovingly) may potentially hurt their child with good intentions. Unpleasant, arrogant, and shockingly dissatisfied children are the ones who have not been disciplined. The idea that children who are given consistent guidelines, restrictions, and goals are accountable, more self-sufficient, are more likely to make healthy decisions, and are more likely to make friends and be happier is one of the main reasons that we need discipline. Treat them with compassion, empathy, and firmness as soon as you see behavioral issues such as deception or backtalk. 'To teach' is the

Latin origin of the term discipline. Disciplining the child means showing them good behavior and self-control. Your child can think about consequences and take responsibility for their own actions with effective and clear discipline. The main goal is to motivate the child to learn to control all their thoughts and behaviors. This is called controlling yourself. At its highest, discipline honors the child with good conduct and, using equal and constructive methods, discourages unacceptable activity. Some parents claim that physical punishment, such as slapping and smacking, or verbal bullying, such as shouting or insulting the child, means discipline. It's not disciplined at all.

The consequences of physical punishment

Kids learn by example. A variety of studies show that the parents are the most important role models in the development of a child. It is important for parents to serve as a model for how they expect their kids to behave. Using physical abuse or causing harm to a child to deter them from misbehaving just shows them that it is okay to fix issues with violence. Children learn how this is done by watching their parents utilize physical violence against them. In addition, punishment can harm the very precious relationship between parent and child.

Reasons for misbehavior

For several reasons, children misbehave:

They are too young to understand that their acts are unacceptable.

They are irritated, distressed, or angry and have no other fair means of voicing their emotions.

Big transitions, such as a family split, a new sibling, or starting education overwhelm them.

When they act appropriately, they do not get your attention.

They believe you have been unjust and want to punish you.

They need a greater degree of autonomy and feel constrained.

Your child's ability to understand

Disciplining a child involves telling the child what behavior is appropriate. The academic capacity of a child grows over time. It is necessary to balance your child's discipline with the capacity of your child to understand. There is no definition of right and wrong for a very young child, such as a kid. Children under three do not misbehave-they have desires, such as hunger and thirst, that they want to fulfill. By modifying behavior, they do not yet adapt to repercussions, and so the same lesson has to be told over and over again, for example,' put your hat on in the heat.' When they choose to go out in the sun without their hats, they are not rebellious – they simply cannot think. Try to convey to your child things in a manner that suits their stage of maturity, and remember to reduce yourself to their physical level as well. In their actions, children act out their emotions, so it is necessary to consider the feelings behind the behavior. You will better solve the root issues once you know the causes behind your child's misbehavior or emotions.

Routines help a child to learn

Kids learn how to act by copying the people around them. When they understand what is expected of them, they excel, and their day has a similar pattern to it. When they know the order of events and can foresee what will happen next, children feel safe. This is the same for reactions to children's behavior. The kid wants to know what the response of the adults will be and if it will be rational and coherent.

Time out for children

For youngsters, spending time alone (taking 'time out') may be a beneficial opportunity for self-reflection before their behavior upsets them or angers their parents. For older children, this is acceptable, as long as the child is not made to feel hurt, ashamed or embarrassed. When kids grow older, the child may learn to carry themselves to their bed under the guidance of helpful reinforcement. For very young kids or children who might see it as humiliation and feel embarrassed or confused for being made to sit in a 'naughty chair' and 'think about what they have done, time out should not be misused.

Time out for parents

If you find yourself getting upset and irritated with your child's actions, you might need to take time out to deal with your own emotions. It could be safer to momentarily detach yourself from a situation you are finding difficult. This could mean making sure that your child is safe for a few minutes and leaving the room. You can also call a friend or a relative to take a break.

Reinforcing good behavior

A kid naturally needs their parents' attention and approval, so it can be used as a more appropriate way for encouraging good behavior in the children

CHAPTER 4: Strategies for Building Trust and Attachment

Developing a stable attachment with your child will support them in several ways. Children with a good parent/guardian bond are more likely to have stronger self-esteem, do well in education, have healthy relationships, and handle stress. Here are four basic ways in which your child will build an attachment.

How to Develop Attachment with a Child

4.1 Be Dependable

There is a desire for your child to see you as a safe place. Whenever he or she is ill, injured, or angry, offer support. If soon as possible, be physically present. They will discover the world on their own while your child feels safe, trusting they can return to you for support and warmth when they need it. Encourage your child to do new things by telling them that they can do it themselves, but if they need to run to you for support, be nearby.

4.2 Be Attentive

Learn to spend one-on-one time with your kid. Discover things that both of you will enjoy, play games together, speak, and listen to their desires. Take the lead of your child on what they need; do not impose a certain type of interaction based on your criteria. Such tasks do not need to take up a lot of time, but it is the love and complete attention that is important. During these encounters, eye contact, comfort and touch, and smiles can help create a connection.

4.3 Be Predictable

To feel safe, children need routines. Having a meal schedule, bedtime, and some other daily activity helps to develop self-discipline and safety for your child. Knowing what happens next helps children to initiate the next step in the routine on their own, fostering their freedom.

4.4 Be Understanding During Separation

It has no effect on your attachment to making your child spend time with another caregiver. In addition to you, your child can establish a bond with another person. Build a goodbye routine while leaving your child with someone else. This predictability causes your kid to feel healthy. It is understandable to be unsure of your kids, but they would probably imitate your actions. Be optimistic to show your kid that it's not annoying. Where necessary, make your child spend time away from you steadily, slowly increasing the length of time you are gone. In order to assist with the change, most daycares encourage parents to remain on-site with their child. A safety blanket or familiar toy helps certain kids. As they mature, developing a close bond with a child is highly helpful for them. Providing safety, comfort, and routine makes it easier for your child to feel comfortable and secure while discovering the world on their own.

4.5 Love

Showering them with affection is one of the most valuable ways to develop a confident relationship with your kids. Offer your children always-present, unconditional love in all of your relationships.

4.6 Communicate

The pillar of faith is communication. The more you speak to your child freely, the more your friendship can improve. Seek out communication opportunities with your child. Ask for their perspective on everything. You will have to learn to listen to them with love, kindness, and without judging.

Be honest

It seems simple, but to build a trustworthy bond, sincerity with your kid is the key. If you're sad, don't tell your kid that you're all right, but be honest and tell your child that you're sad. You don't have to tell the details to your kid as to why you're upset, so you have to be truthful with your feelings. If your kid inquires you a question about which you have no answer, let her know that you are uncertain. You can tell her you're going to have to ponder about it, or you can ask her to assist you in finding out the answer to her question.

Support honesty

Support honesty is a crucial part of building a bond of confidence with your kid. You have to let them know when your girls do something wrong because while the behavior might be frustrating, lying about it creates it even worse. When they've been truthful and tell you the truth about a case, you can really commend your children. It is important that your kid understands that you value their honesty is important.

Avoid promises

You need to avoid making promises with your kids. Sometimes, promises are impossible to fulfill. There are also conditions that result in arrangements needing to change; it is easier to justify these changes if you have not promised anything.

Be an ideal

Your kid watches whatever you do. Their impressions of you cause them to influence their views about whether you are reliable. It's important that you role model the habits you want your kid to follow. For instance, you should make your bed every day if you want your kid to make his bed every day, too. If you want your child to talk to someone with dignity, you should also do the same. The more that your kid sees you following the principles and laws you teach, the more they will trust you and have faith in you.

CHAPTER 5: Tips for Inflexible children

Kids who are inflexible can be bossy. In the narrative they build together, they can dictate to their friends what part they can play and which blocks they can read. While these habits are "unacceptable," it is important to understand that they are mechanisms of coping that help alleviates the tension and anxiety of not being in charge. It requires time and maturity to help inflexible children develop tolerance, but it is profoundly necessary for their total functioning in this dynamic environment. The tips for teaching flexibility to kids are given below:

5.1 Authenticate your child's experience and emotions

Understand, emotions are never an issue — it is normally what children do with their emotional state that can be troublesome. The more you understand the feeling that drives their actions, the more they are going to learn to do it in more productive ways.

5.2 Set the boundary peacefully and lovingly

But Grandma went to the doctor, and it took longer than anticipated for the appointment.

So, I'm here to get you. Ignore his efforts to make you fight, but don't ignore him. You might start sharing a funny story, turning on the music he loves, or dreaming about what you will do together when you reach home, even though he's kicking and crying as you strap him into the car seat, to reassure him that you are ready to contribute in positive means but would not keep a bad relationship going.

5.3 Demonstrate perspective-taking

When you correctly set boundaries and do not give in to the unrealistic expectations of your child, you make your child understand the world from the point of view of other people and take their wishes and emotions into account. For instance: "Teddy, I know that you need me to read this book, but Joey is restless and needs to change his diaper." When he's all set, I'll read to you. Then disregard his antics, change the diaper of baby, then when you're done, re-engage Teddy. Let him know that he's been doing a fine job of waiting (even though he's been crying all the time) and that you can read the book now. The goal is to rely on the fact that he stayed alive the wait—the result you want to support—and not pay heed to the actions that are intended to derail you and make you conform to his specifications.

5.4 Model flexibility

In your daily experiences, highlight ways that you are flexible. "I can't find my favorite glasses. I guess I'm going to have to be flexible to wear this one instead." The restaurant shall not open before night. We're going to have to be versatile to find another spot to eat.

5.5 Recognize and give positive comments when your kid is flexible

You gave Harry the tunnel he needed for his car and, instead, you took the bridge. Being agile, you did a fine job! "You wanted to go on the swing, but all of them were taken, so instead, you played in the sandbox." Nice jobs to be versatile! "You wanted to turn on the tap water for the bath, but mother had already done the same. You were frustrated, but you were able to comfort yourself and have a pleasant tub-time.

Conclusion

Happiness and satisfaction, in a world that emphasizes success, are equally important and advantageous. On average, happier individuals are more effective at both work and love than unhappy individuals. They get greater reviews of performance, have more prestigious work, and earn higher incomes. They are more likely to get married, and they are happier with their marriage after they're married. Statistically, happier parents are more likely to have happy children, and no genetic component has been identified to date for the said fact. Hang out with friends or family members who are likely to laugh at themselves because humor is infectious. In order to lighten the mood, their laughing will make you laugh too. Neuroscientists assume that in an area of the brain, hearing another human laugh activates mirror neurons that make listeners sound as though they are truly laughing themselves. Many parents put a priority on the marks and extracurricular activities of their children, such as ensuring that kids study, do their assignments, and get to soccer practice or dance classes on time. Yet all too often, we fail to devote time and resources to cultivating another aspect of the growth and development of children, one that is just as important as becoming a decent person and maybe perhaps more important. The value of countering the prevalent messages of immediate consumerism, gratification, and selfishness that are present in our culture may be simple to overlook. It can be very tough to work out how to make our children happy now. But what's much more important is to teach them values that for the rest of their lives will make them happier. Fortunately, over the past decade, a lot of research has been done on this subject. Parents ought to have a good bond with each other. It may sound like a no-brainer that it would lead to a happy child to have a stronger relationship with your child, but you're most likely thinking about the stage at which the child has become old enough to talk to you and understand you. This idea, however, turns out to start as early as childhood. One of the essential skill sets we can pass on to our children is social skills, as they impact everything they're going to do, from their friendships and intimate relationships to their jobs.

CPSIA information can be obtained
at www.ICGtesting.com
Printed in the USA
BVHW051733090321
602113BV00002B/125